Fun Letter Tracing All rights reserved.

More Kid's Activities Books
Visit : K-Imagine-Pub.com

Time to be a unicorn coloring book for kids

Dot to Dot Zombie coloring book

1-10 Dot to dot airplane coloring book

Dot to dot Things That Go!

1-10 Dot-to-Dots and coloring book

1-10 Dot to dot Magical Unicorn coloring book

1-10 Dot to dot Magical Unicorn

Dot to Dot Book for Kids Ages 3+

Dot to dot space travel coloring book for kids

Airplane Coloring Book

Things That Go Coloring Book

1-20 Dot to Dot coloring book for kids

A is for Airplane

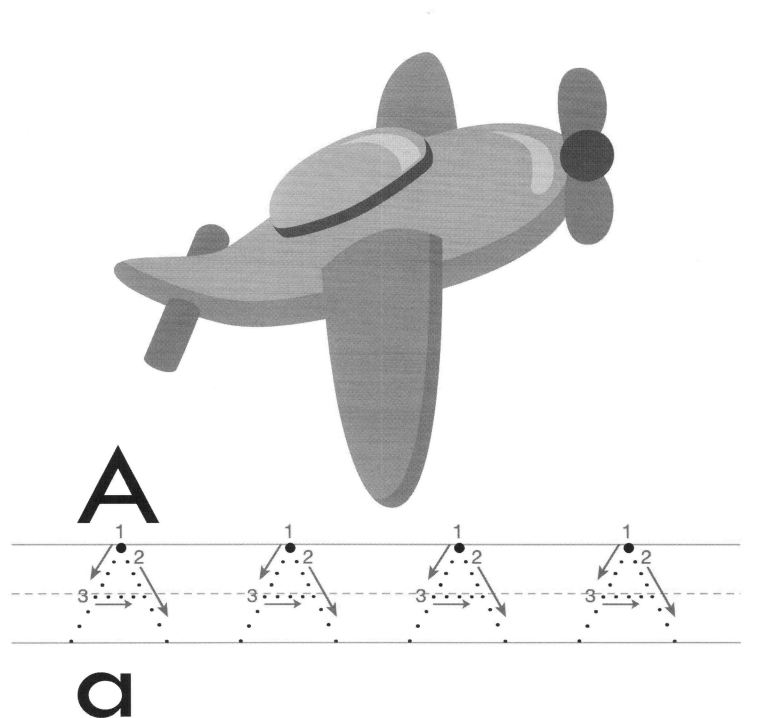

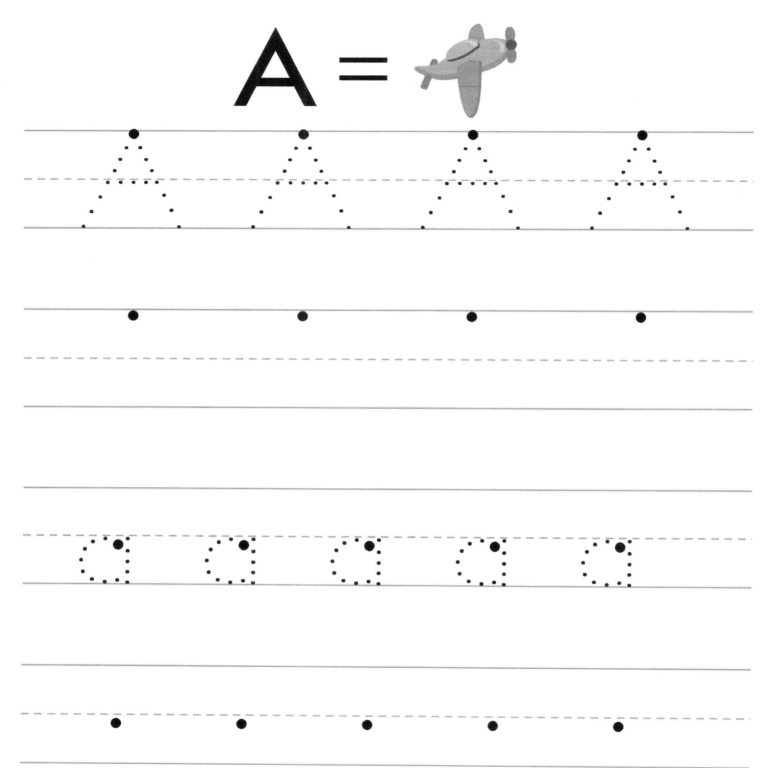

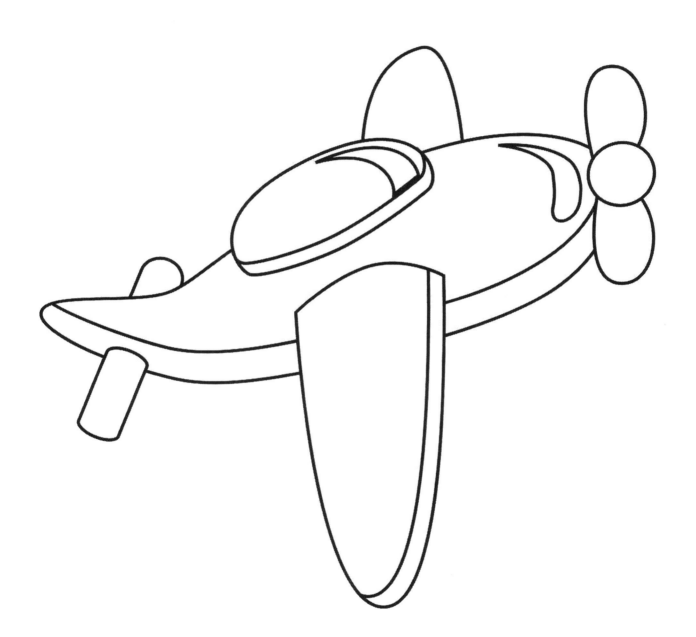

B is for Ball

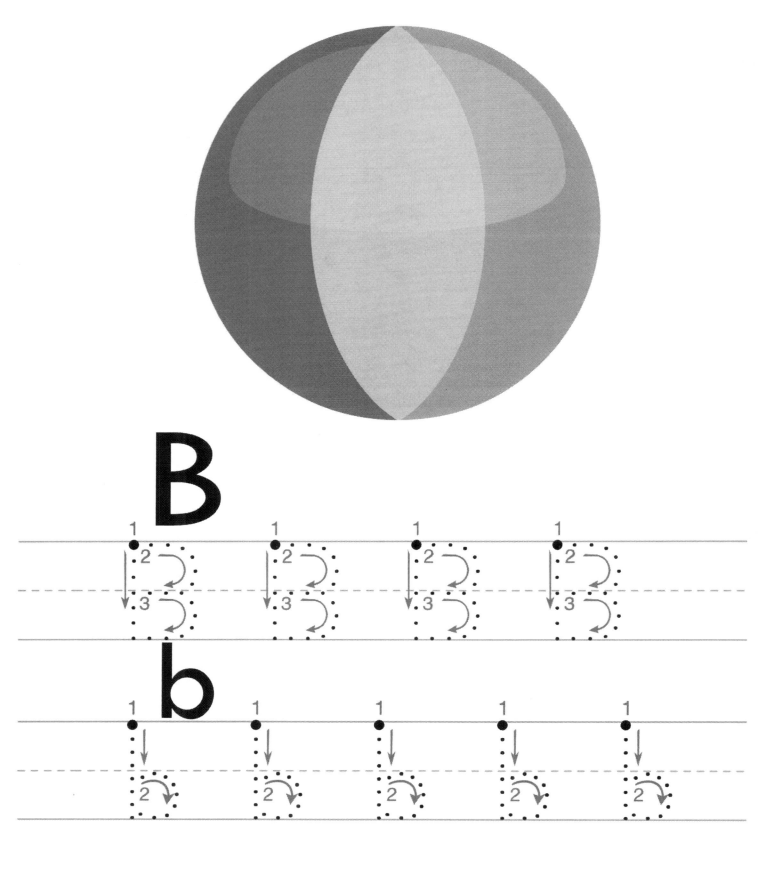

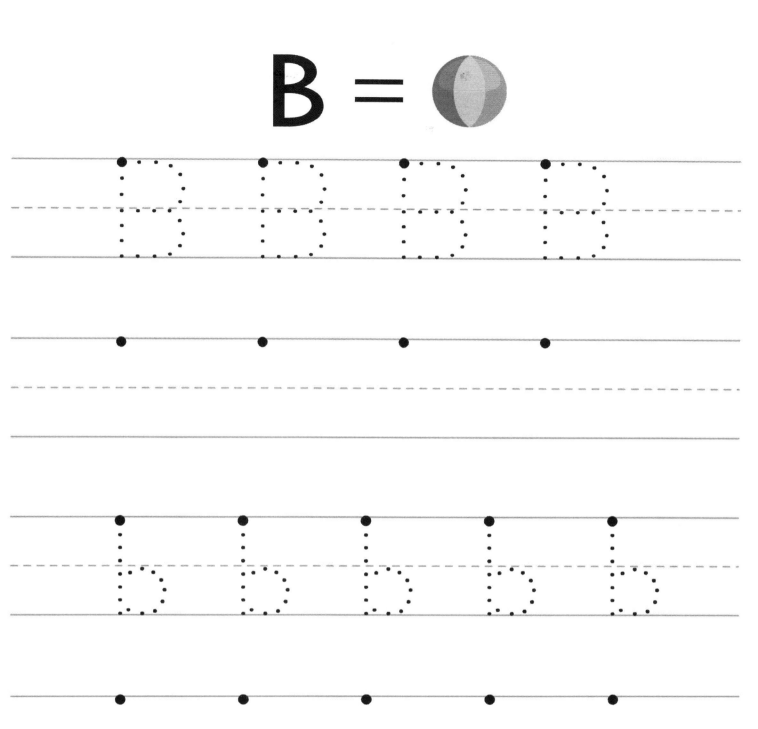

B =

b =

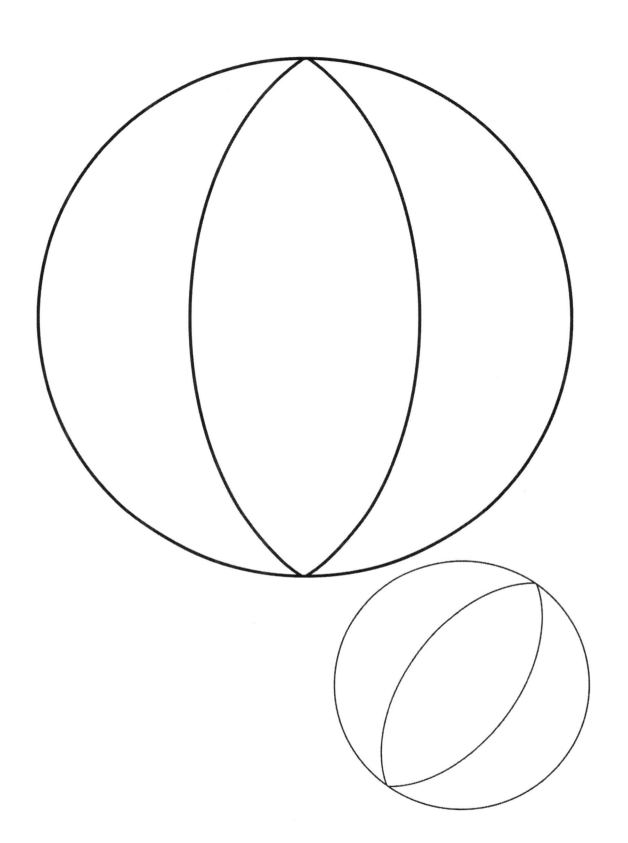

C is for Cap

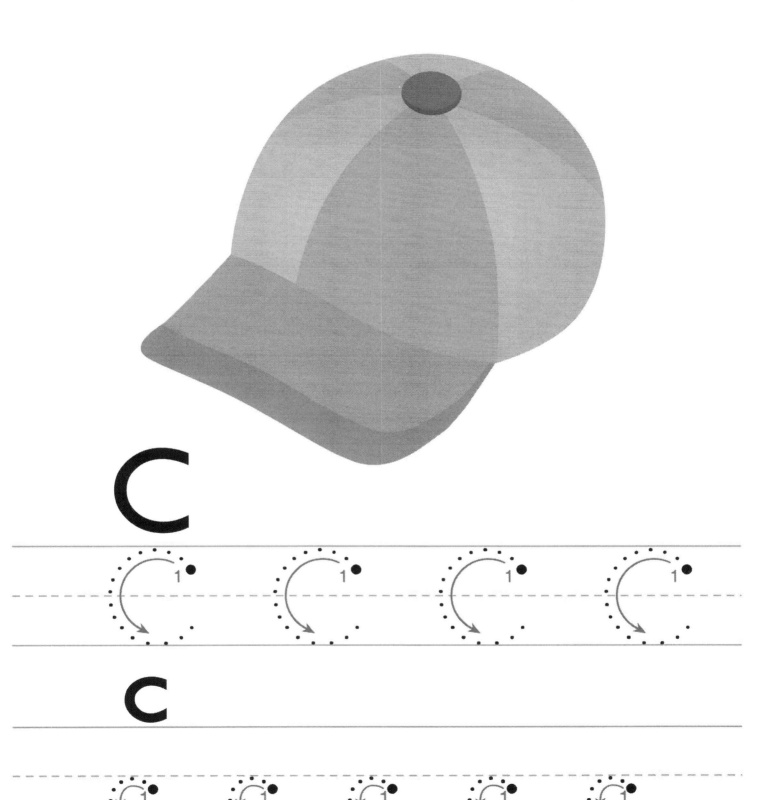

C

c

C =

C =

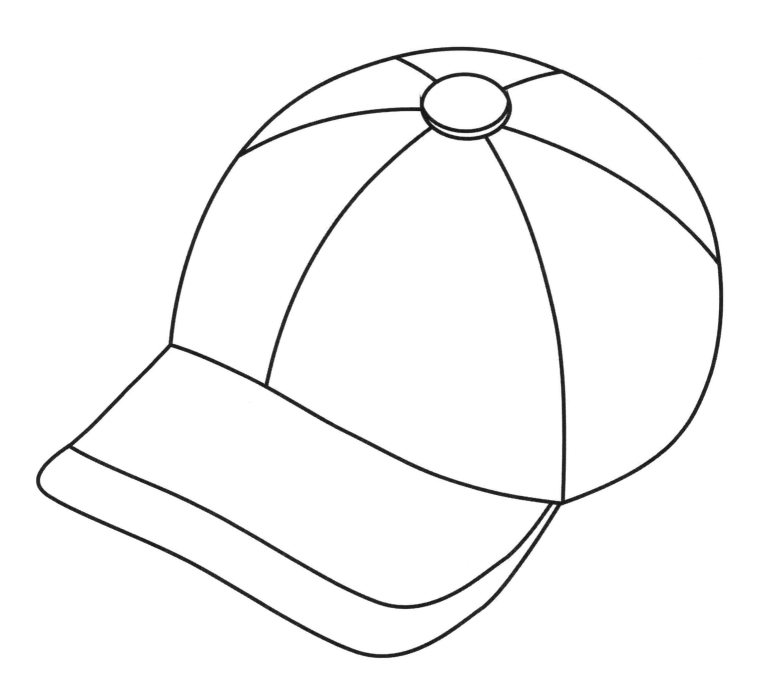

D is for Dog

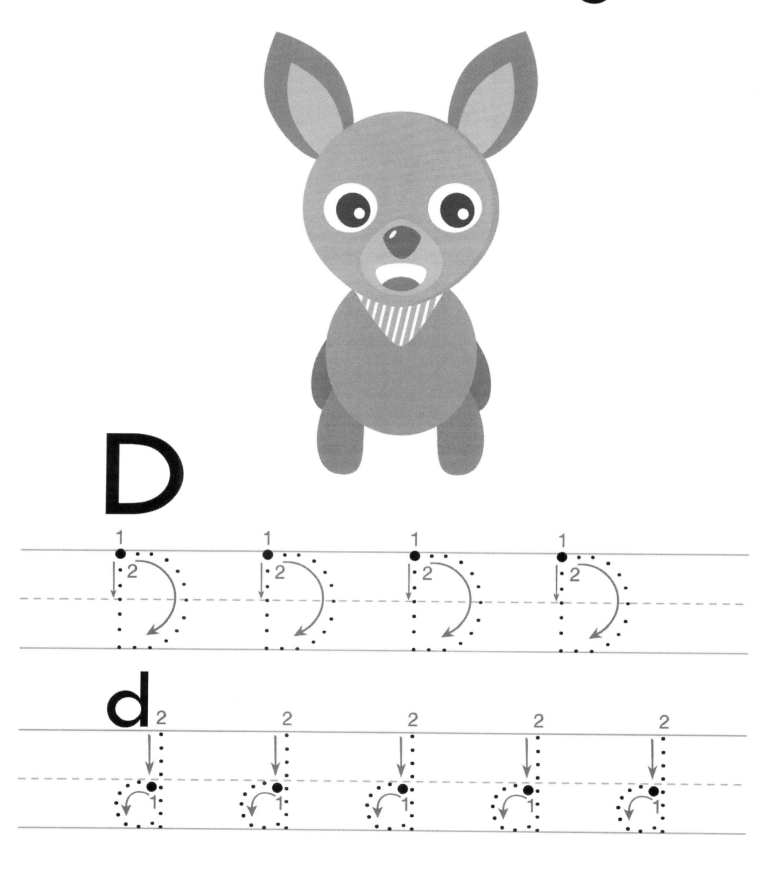

D =

d =

E is for Elephant

E

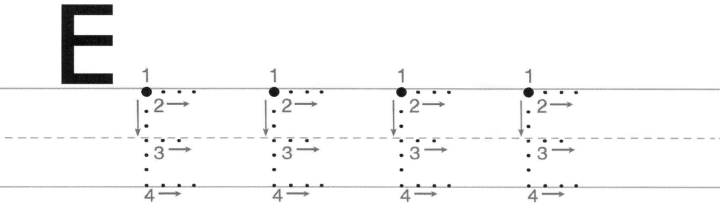

e

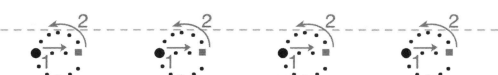

E =

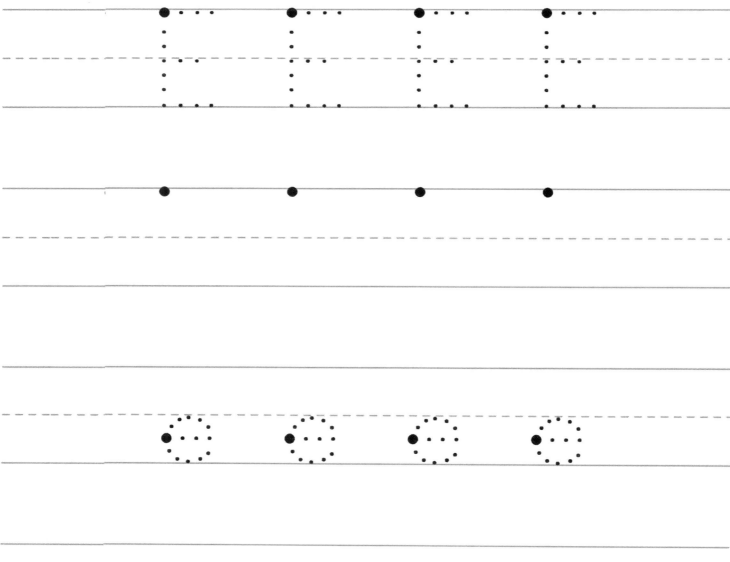

e =

F is for Frog

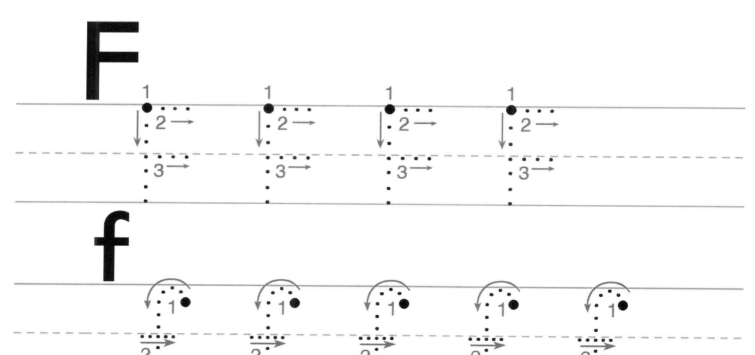

F =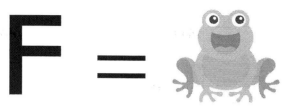

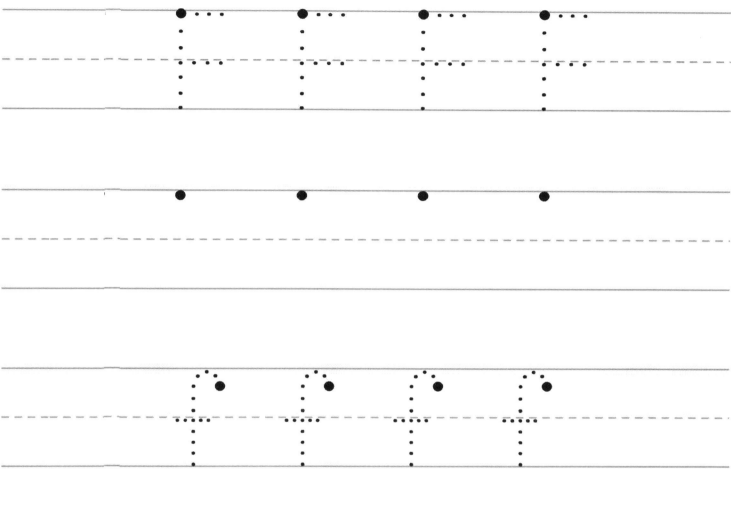

f =

G is for Girl

G

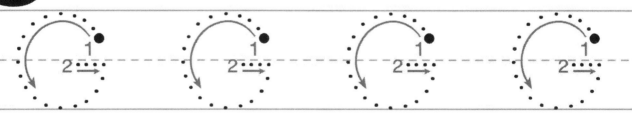

g

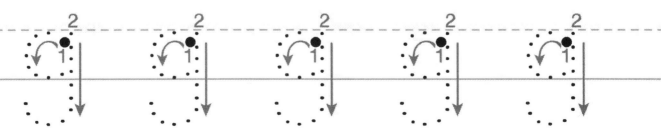

G =

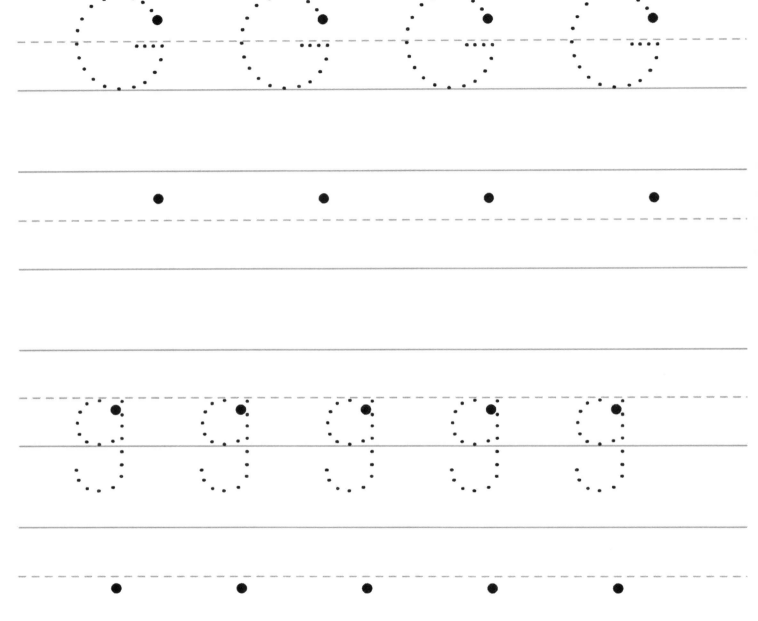

g =

H is for Hammer

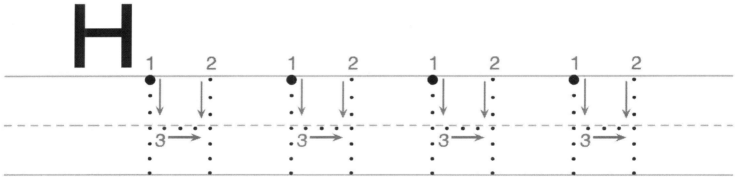

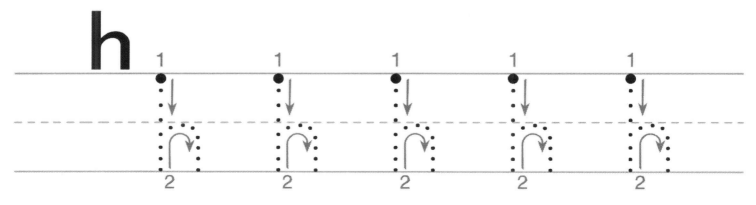

H =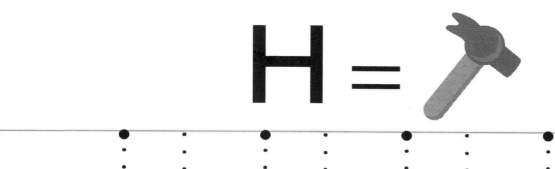

H H H H

h h h h h

h =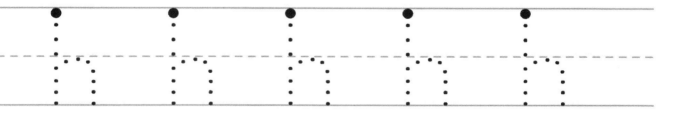

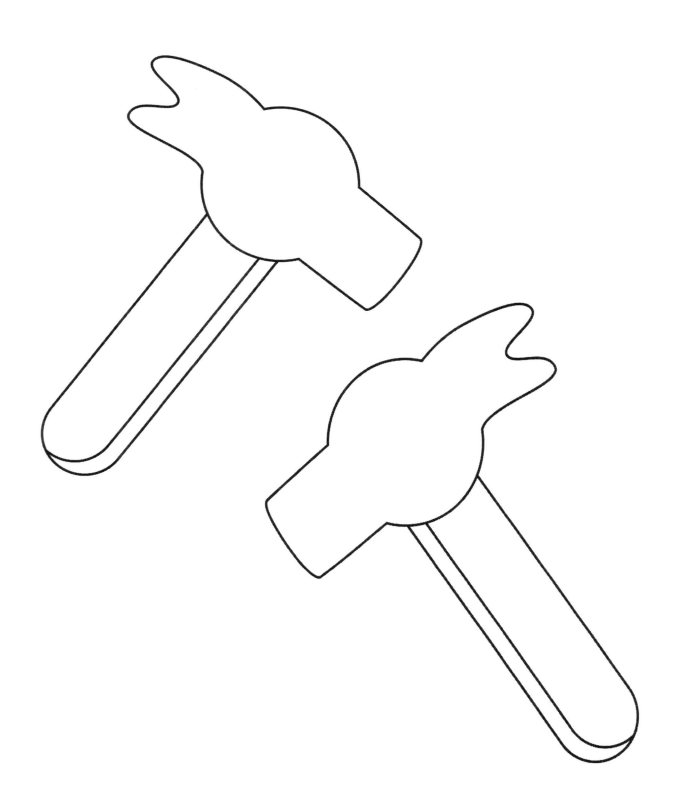

I is for Ice cream

I

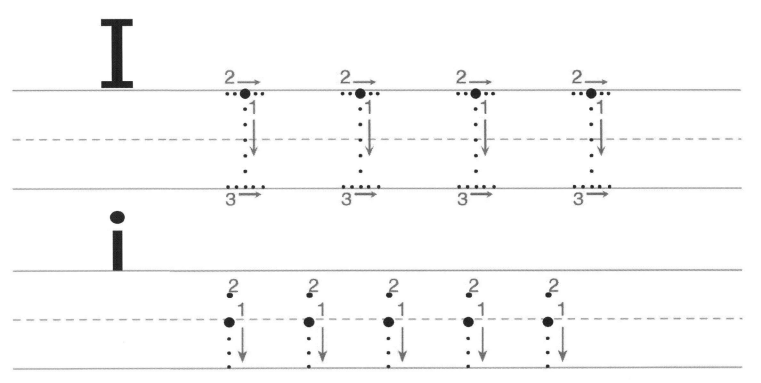

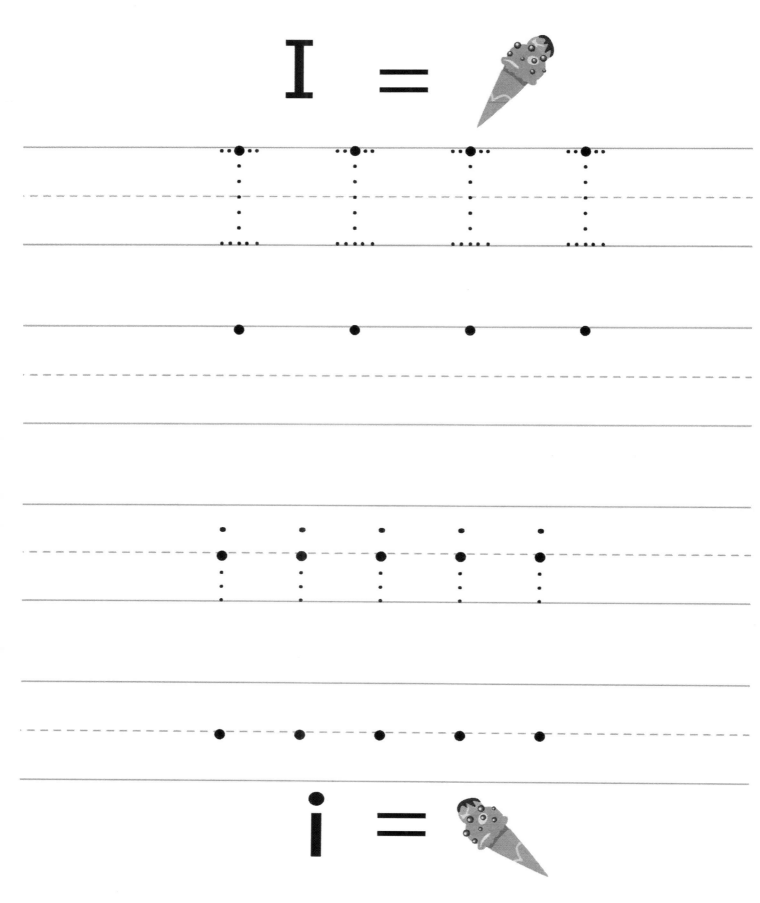

J is for Jar

J

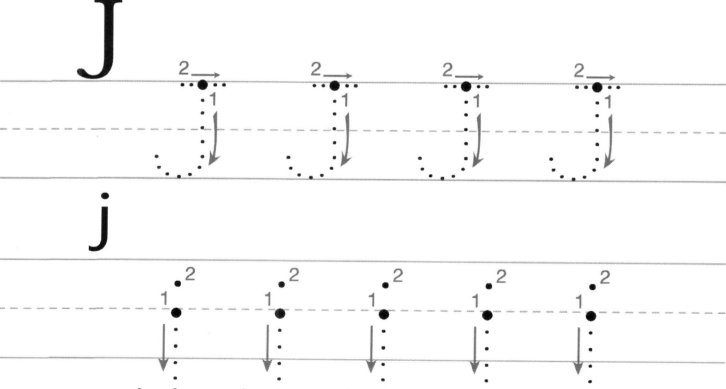

j

J =

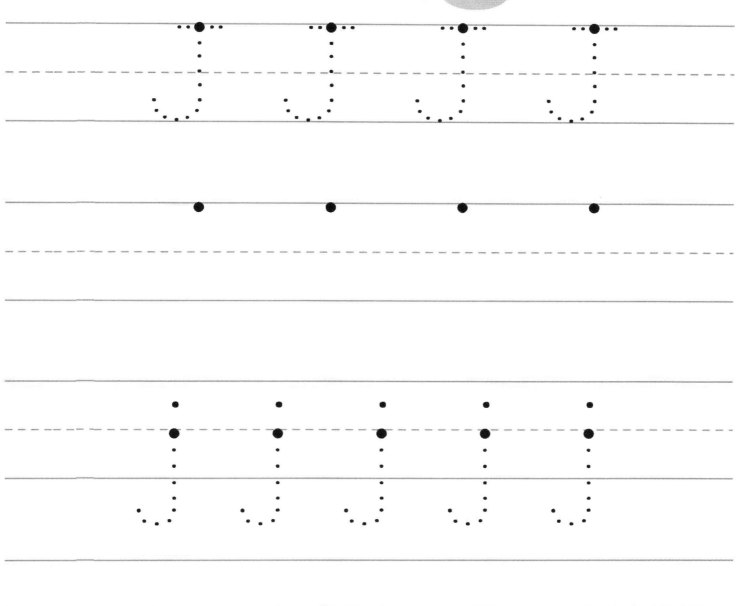

j =

K is for Kiwi

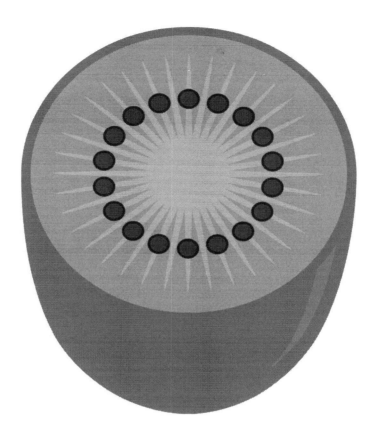

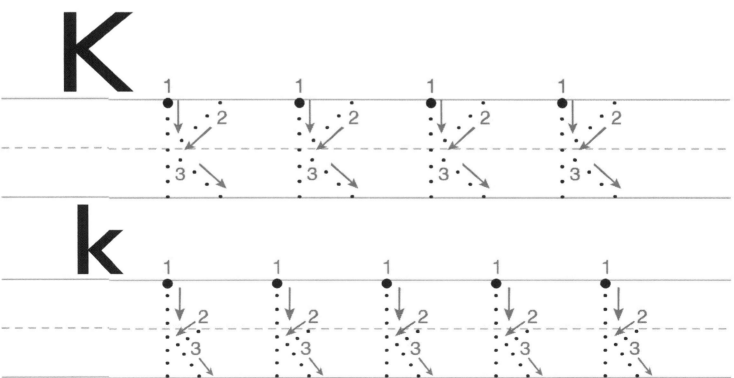

K =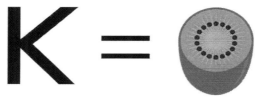

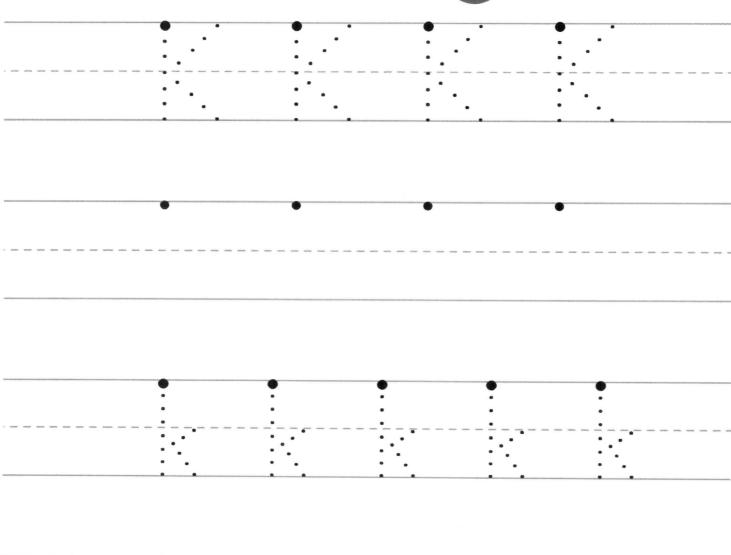

k =

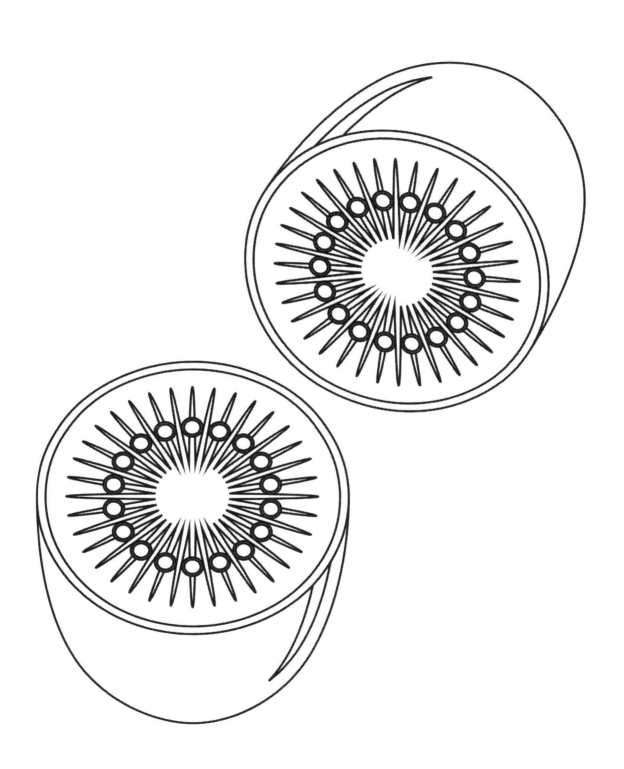

L is for Ladybug

L

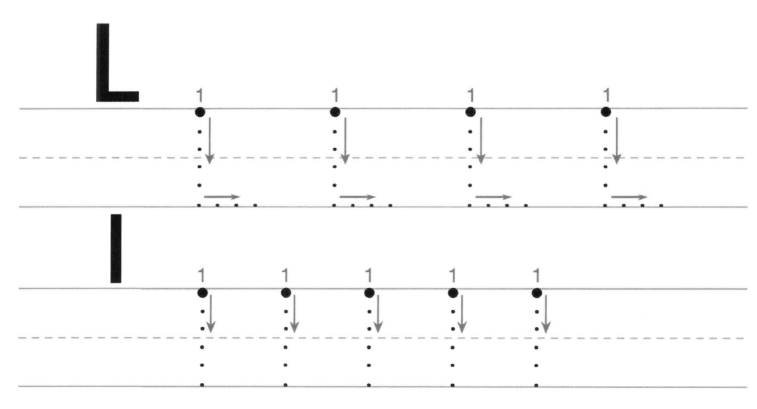

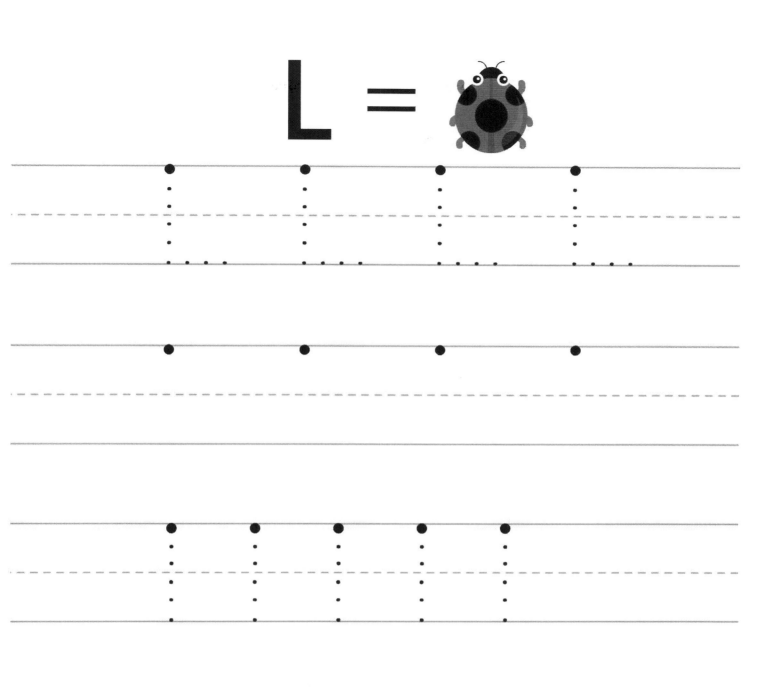

M is for Monkey

M

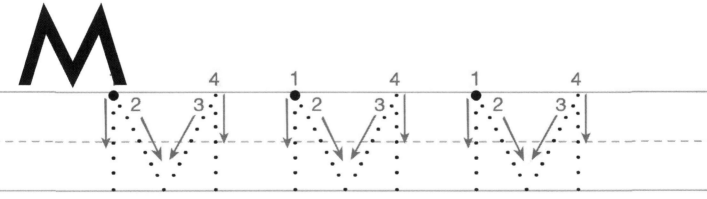

m

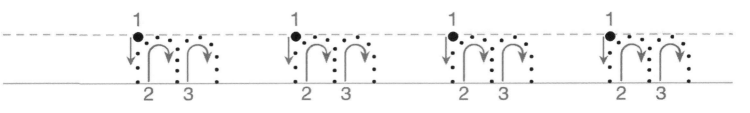

M =

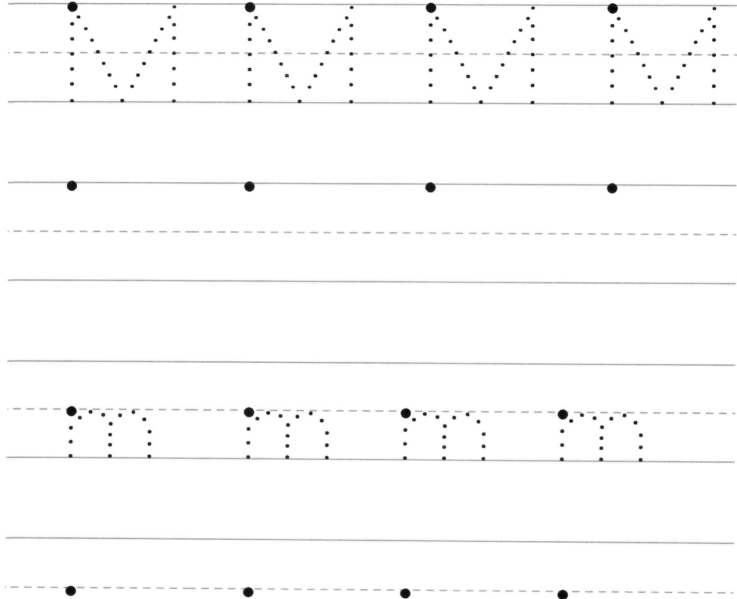

m =

N is for Nail

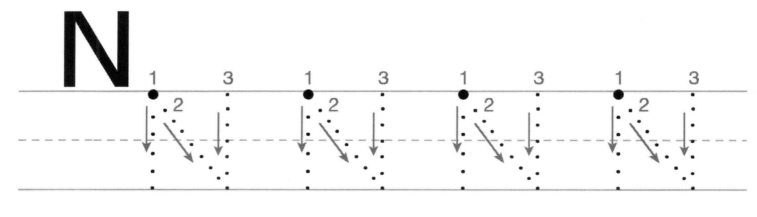

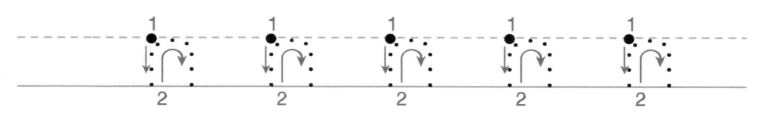

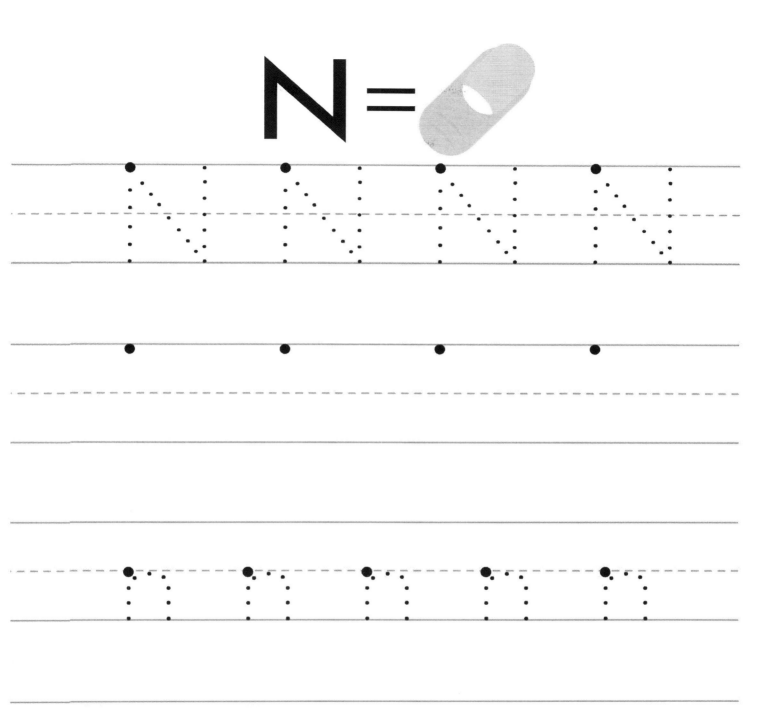

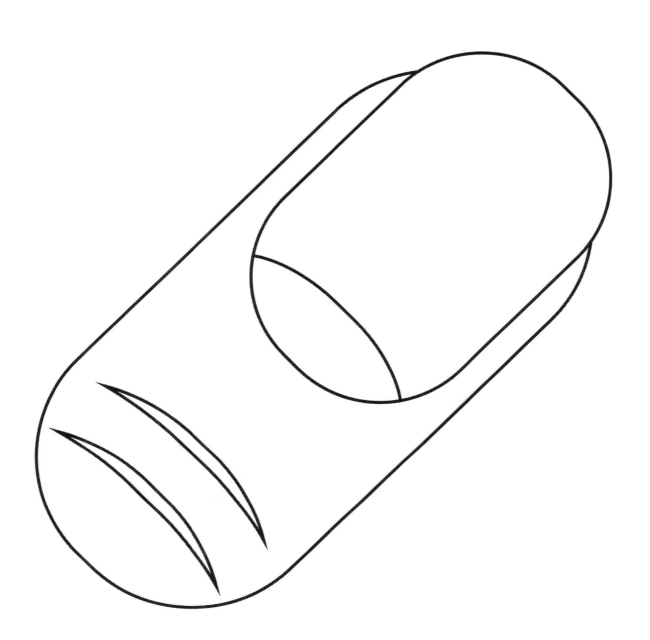

O is for Octopus

O

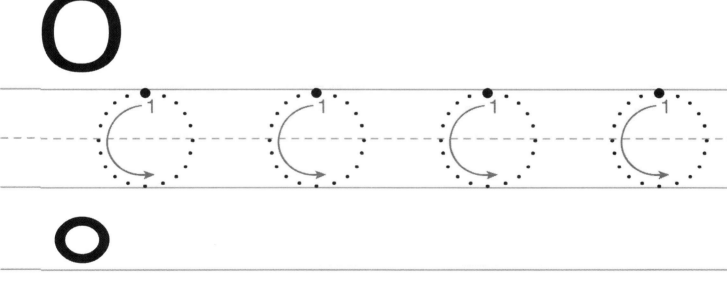

O

P is for Pencil

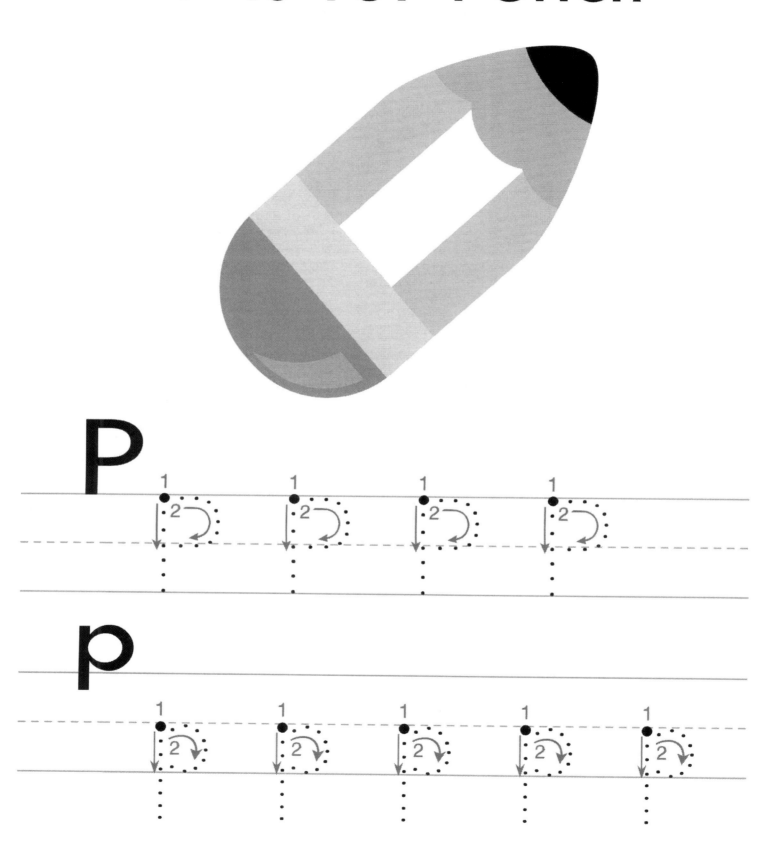

P =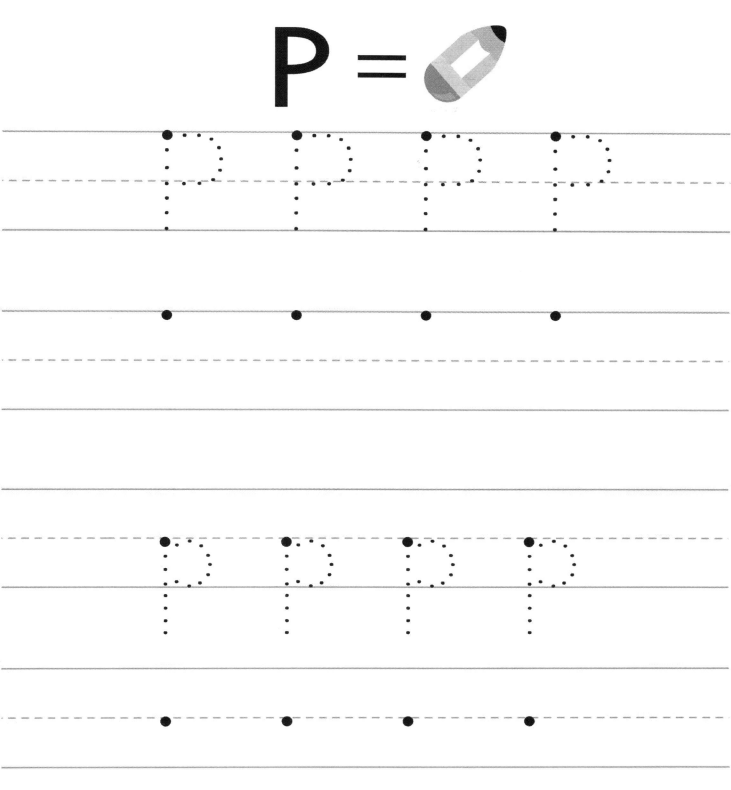

p =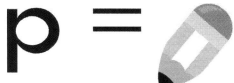

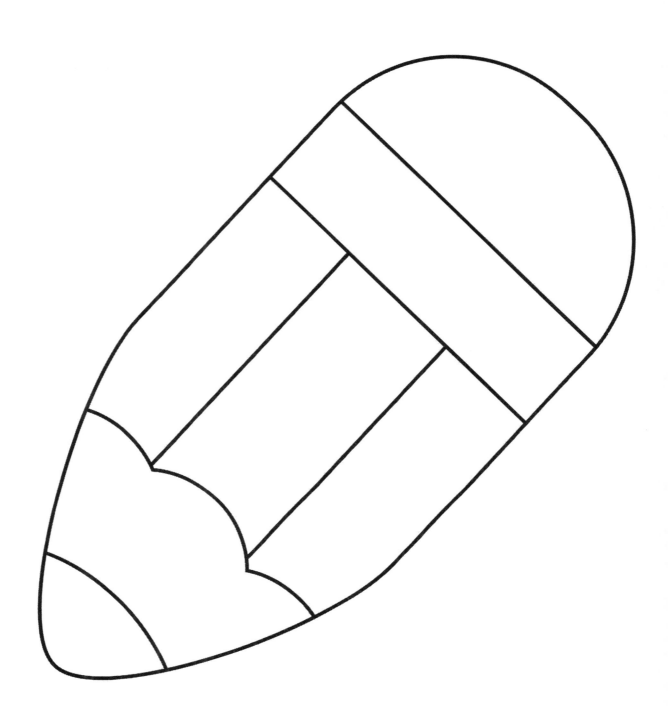

Q is for Quail

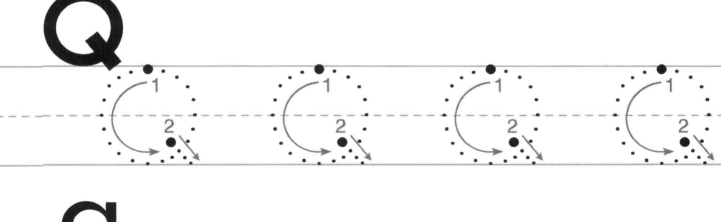

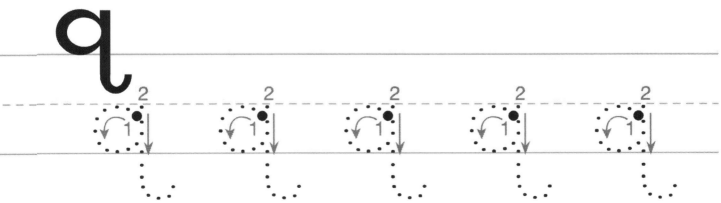

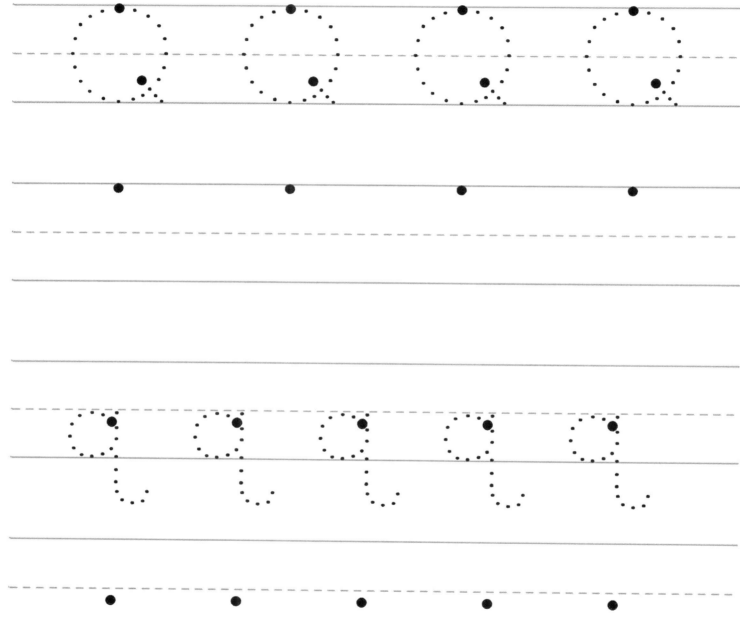

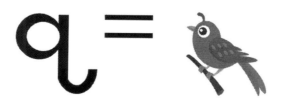

R is for Rocket

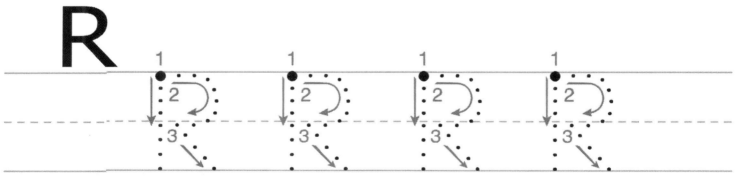

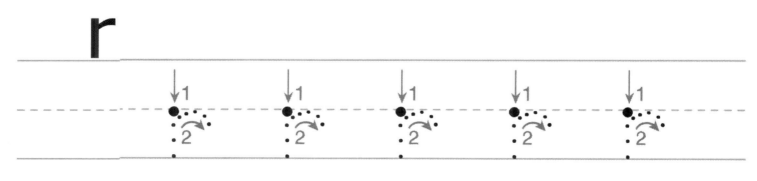

R =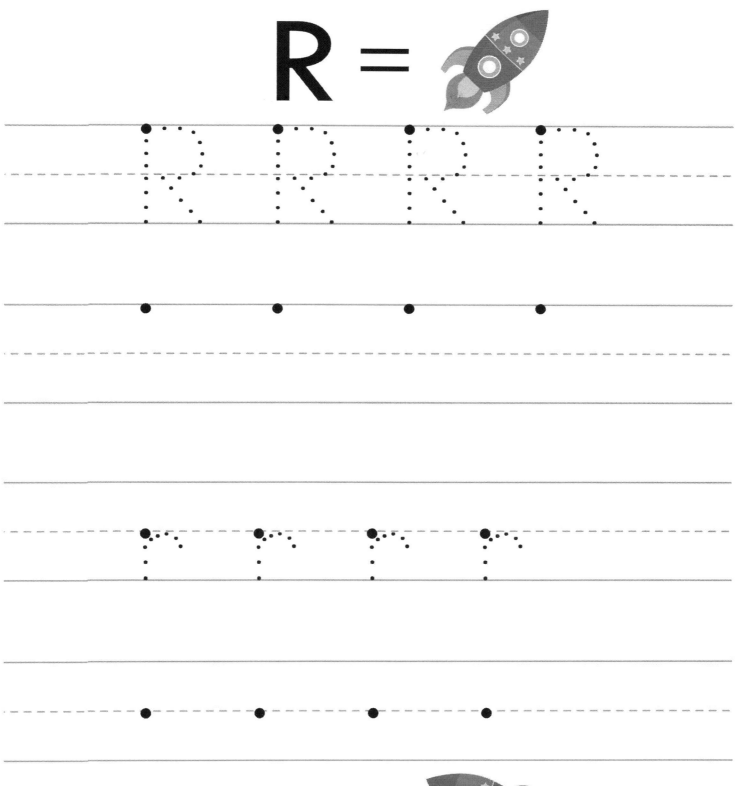

r =

S is for Star

S

s

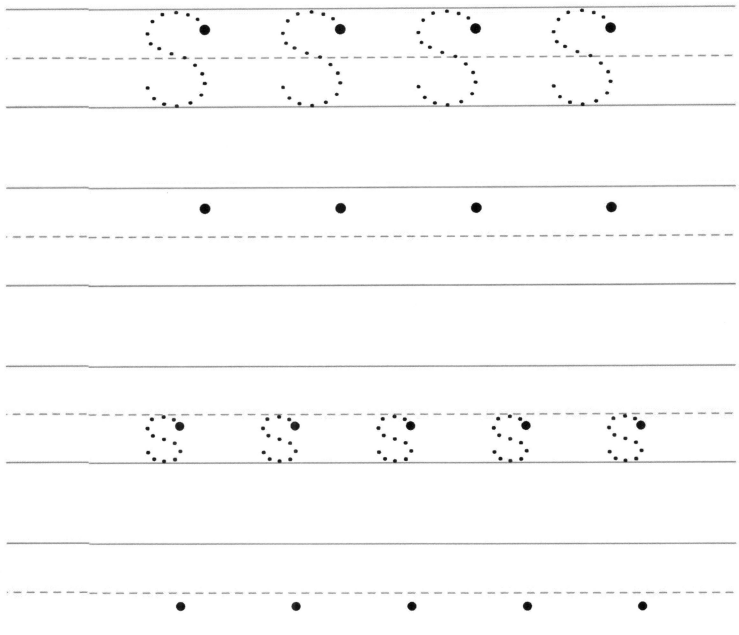

T is for Telephone

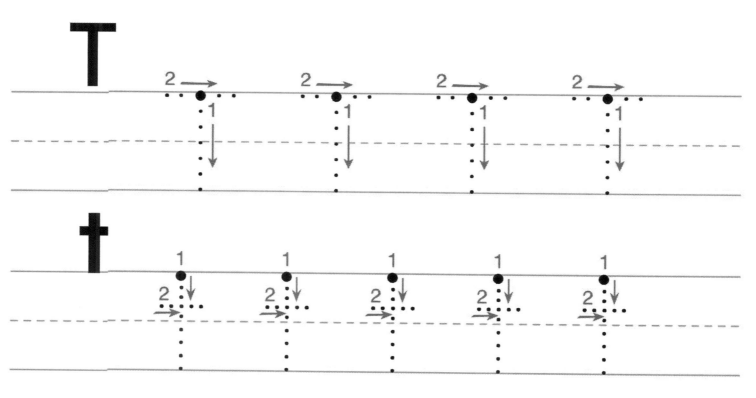

T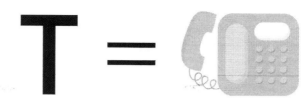

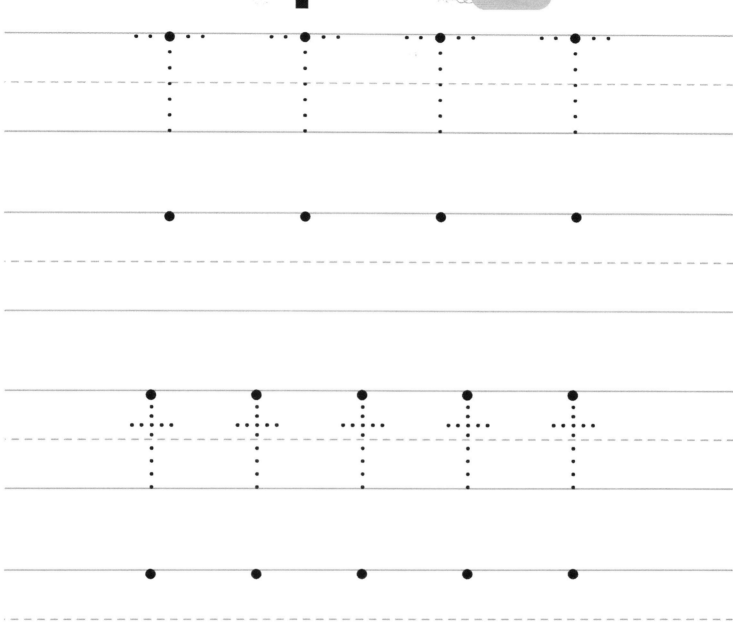

t

U is for Umbrella

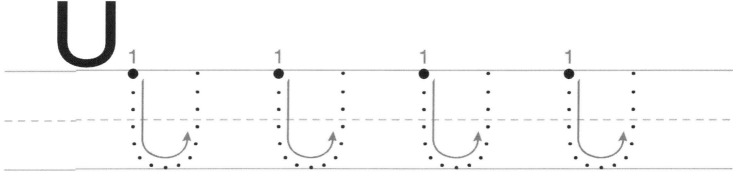

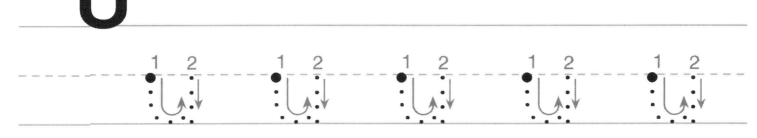

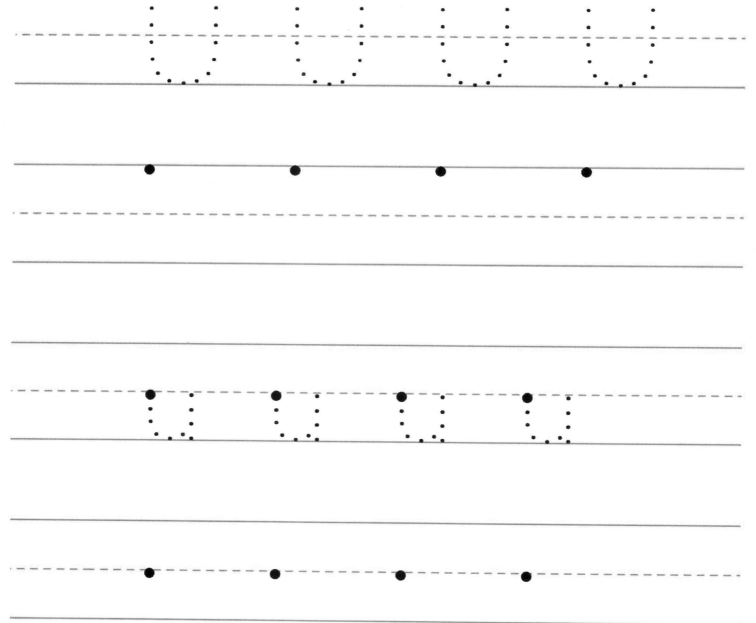

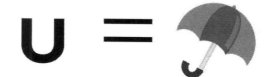

V is for Van

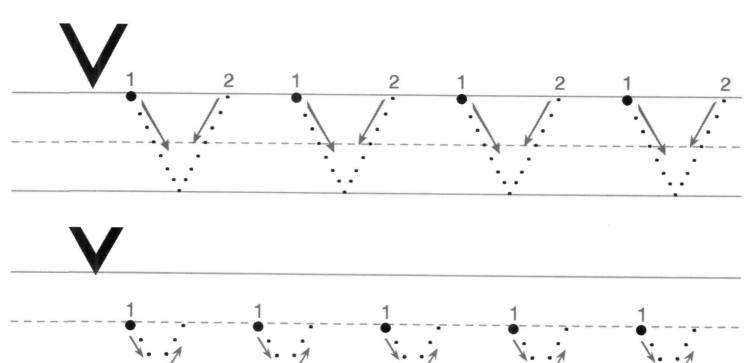

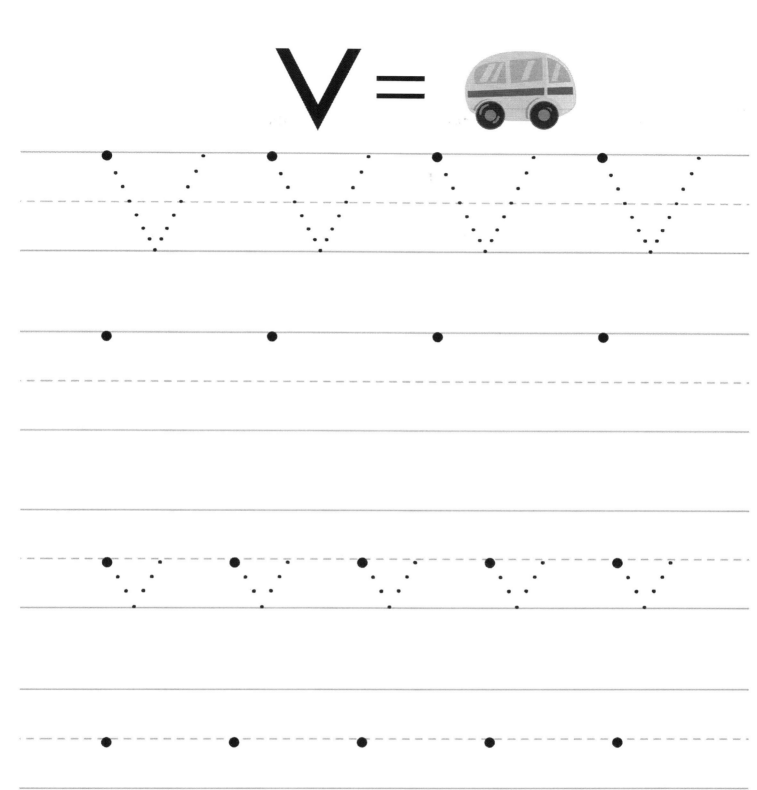

V =

v =

W is for Worm

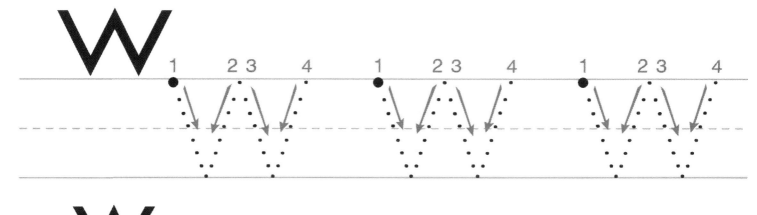

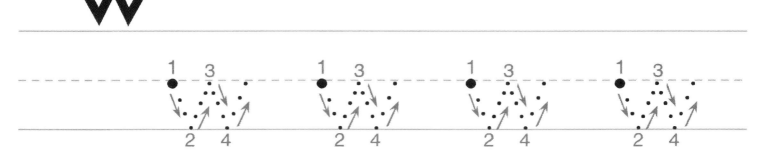

W =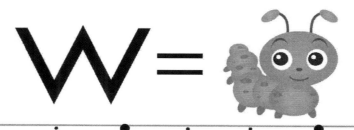

w =

X is for X-ray

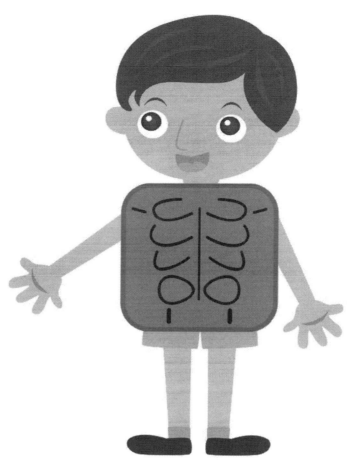

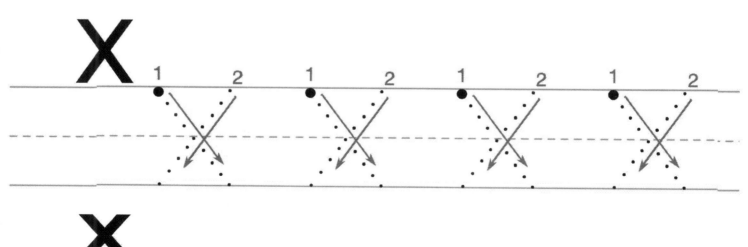

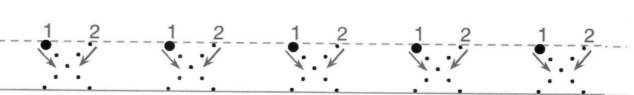

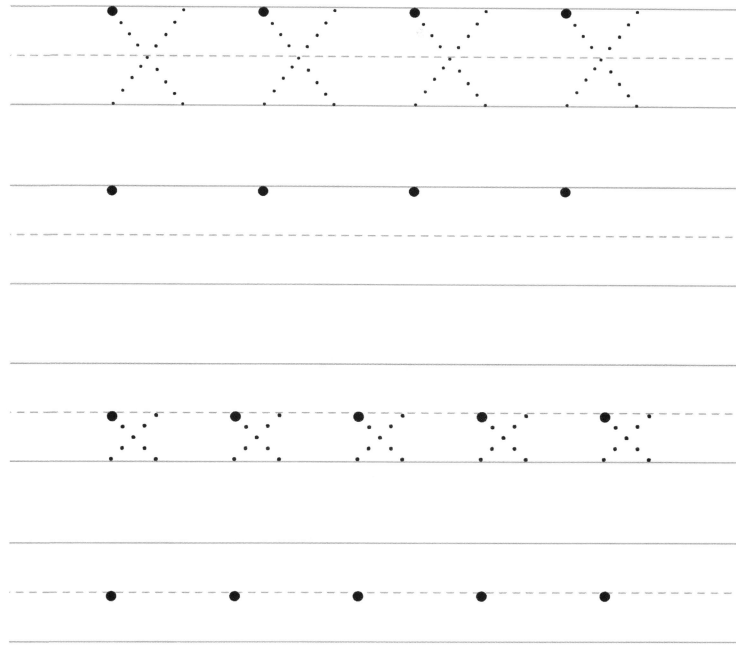

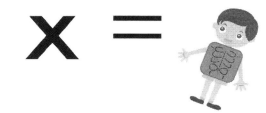

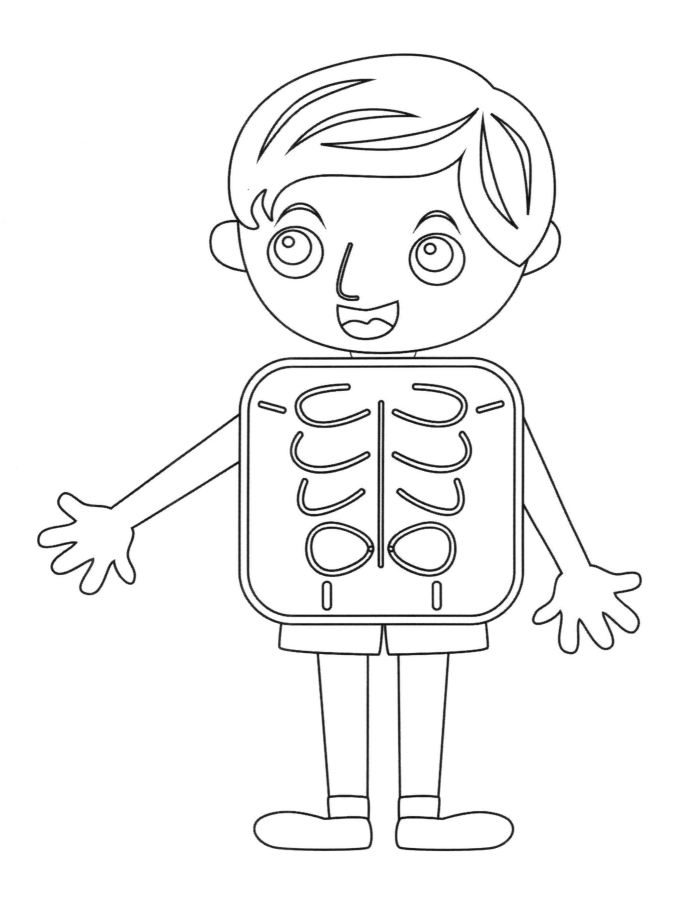

Y is for Yo-Yo

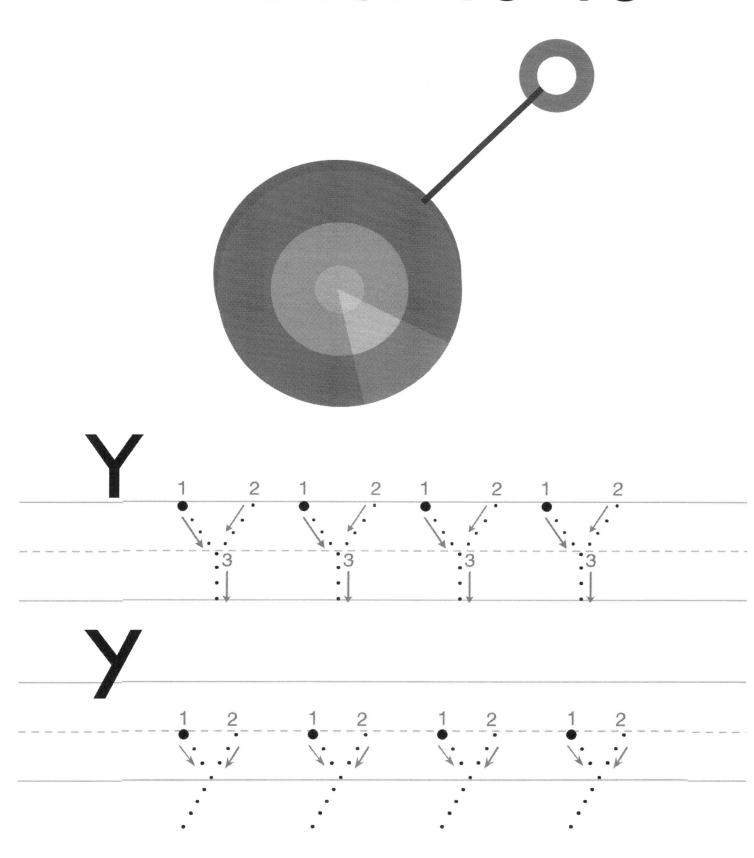

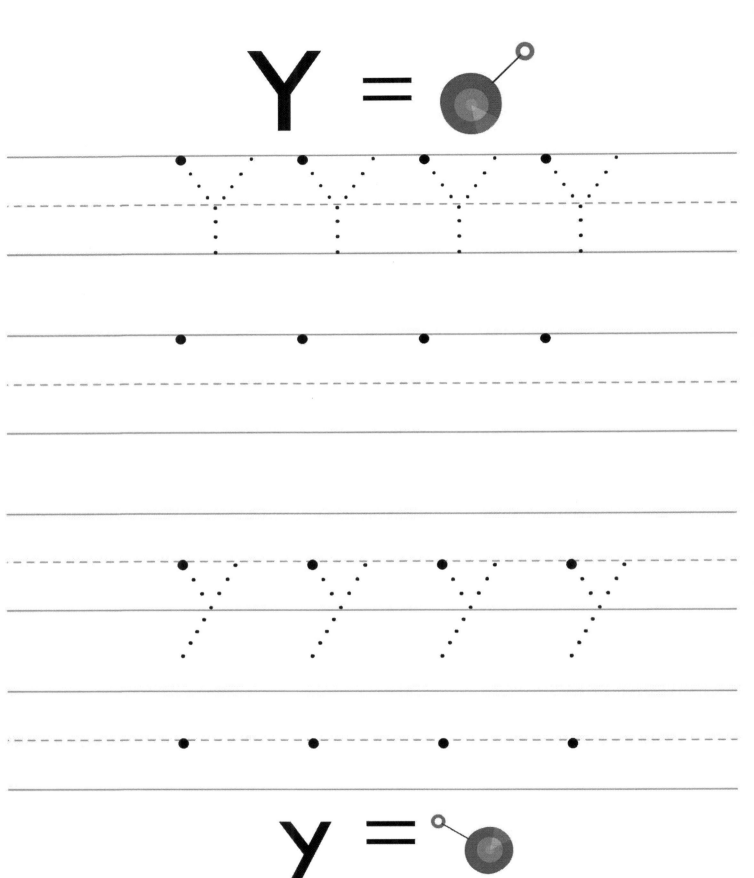

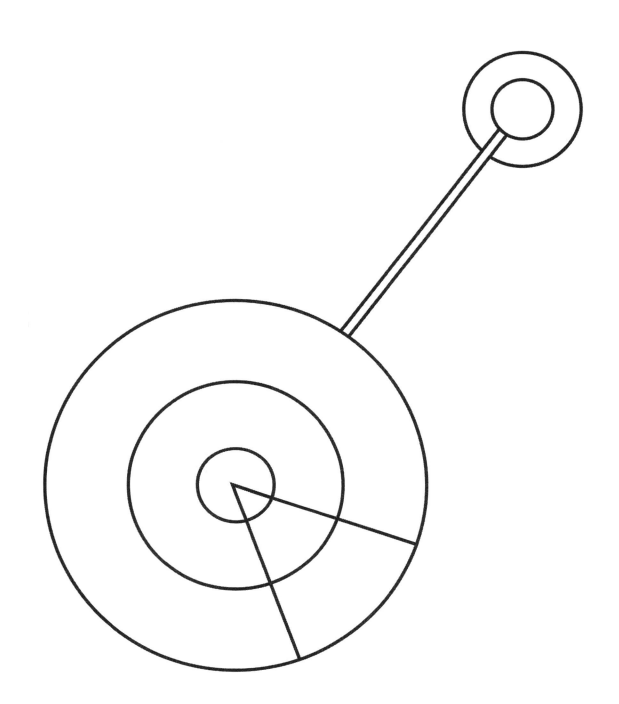

Z is for Zebra

Z =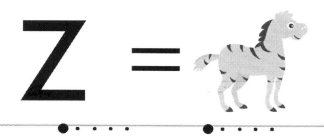

z =

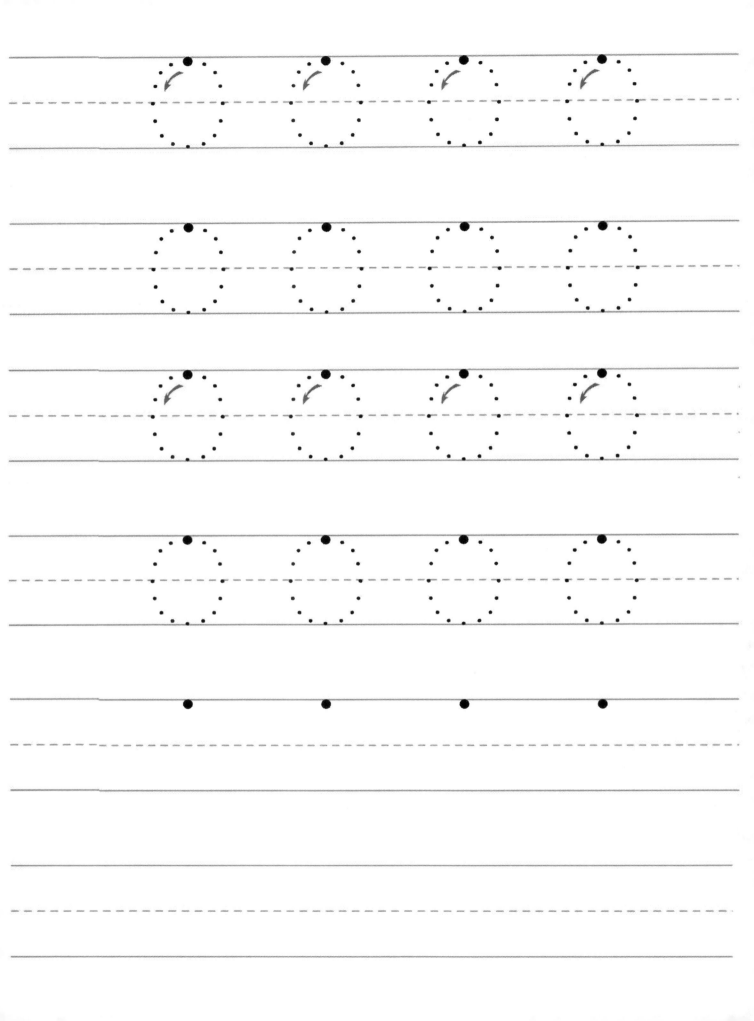

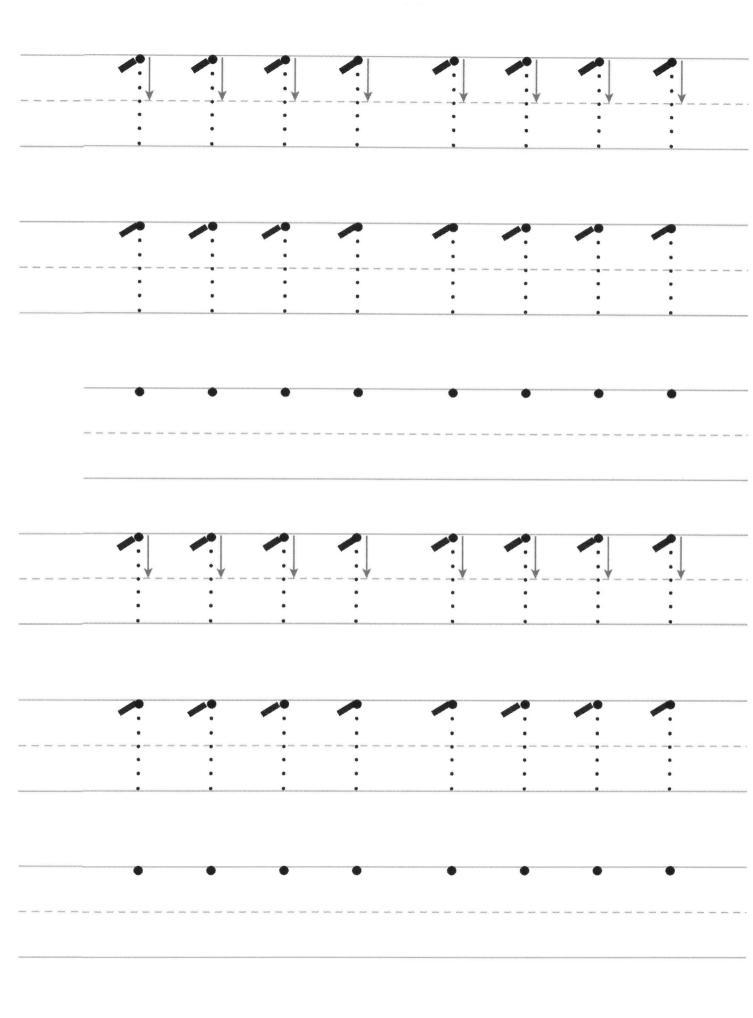

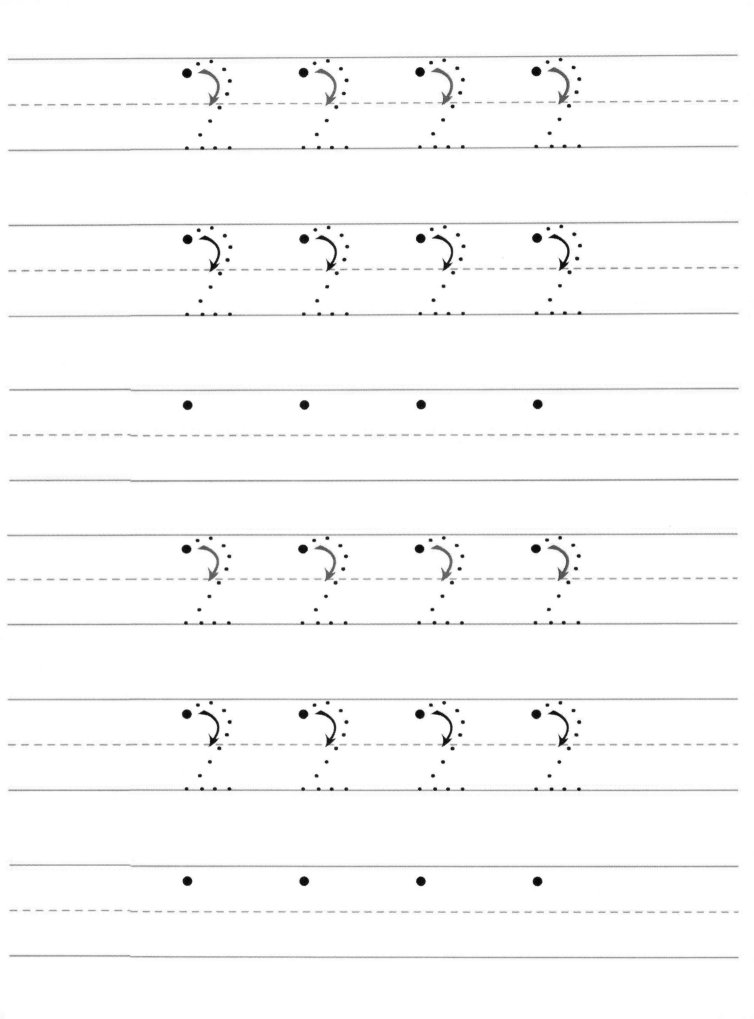

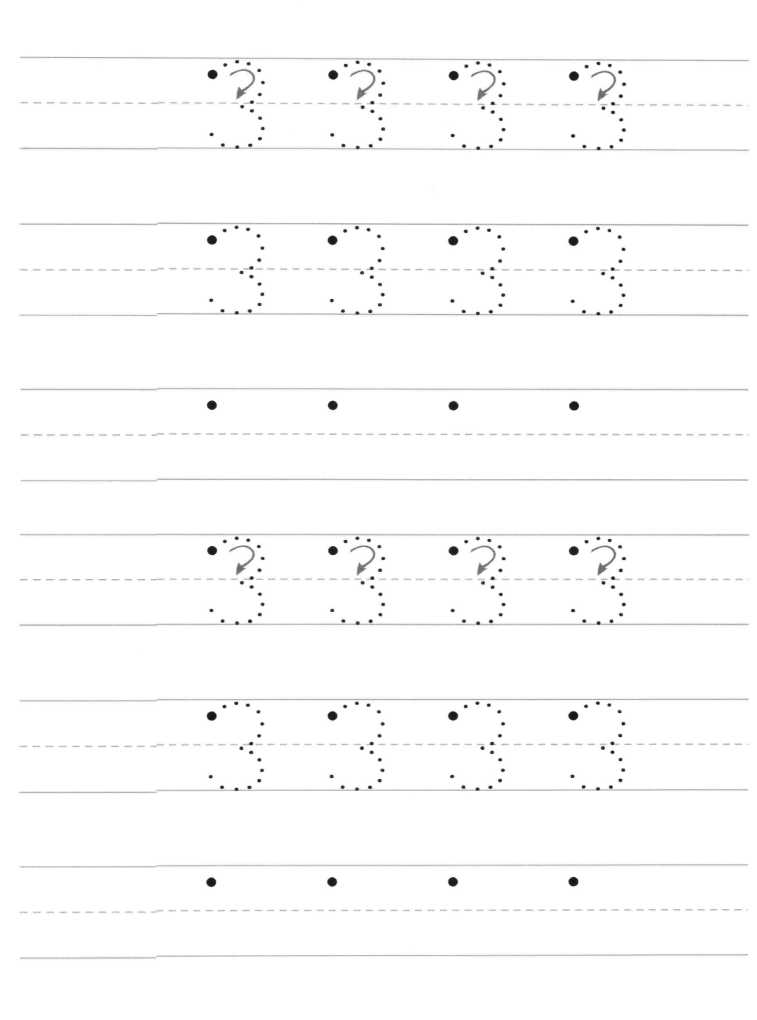

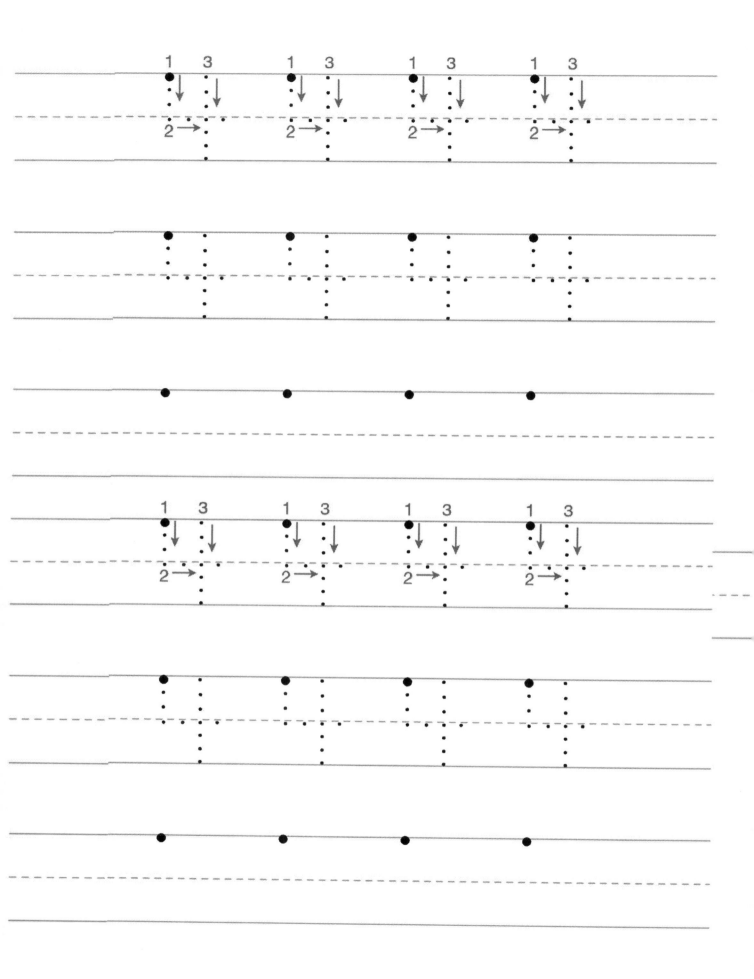

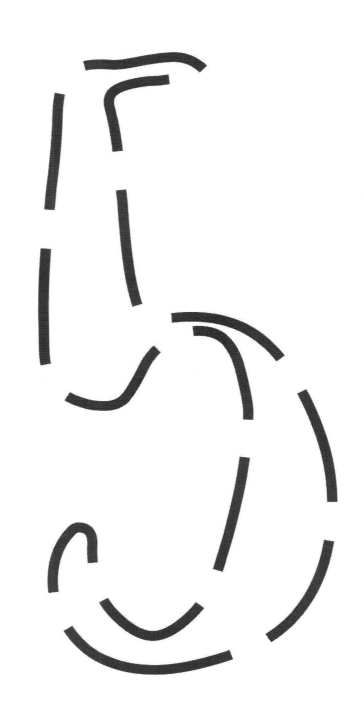

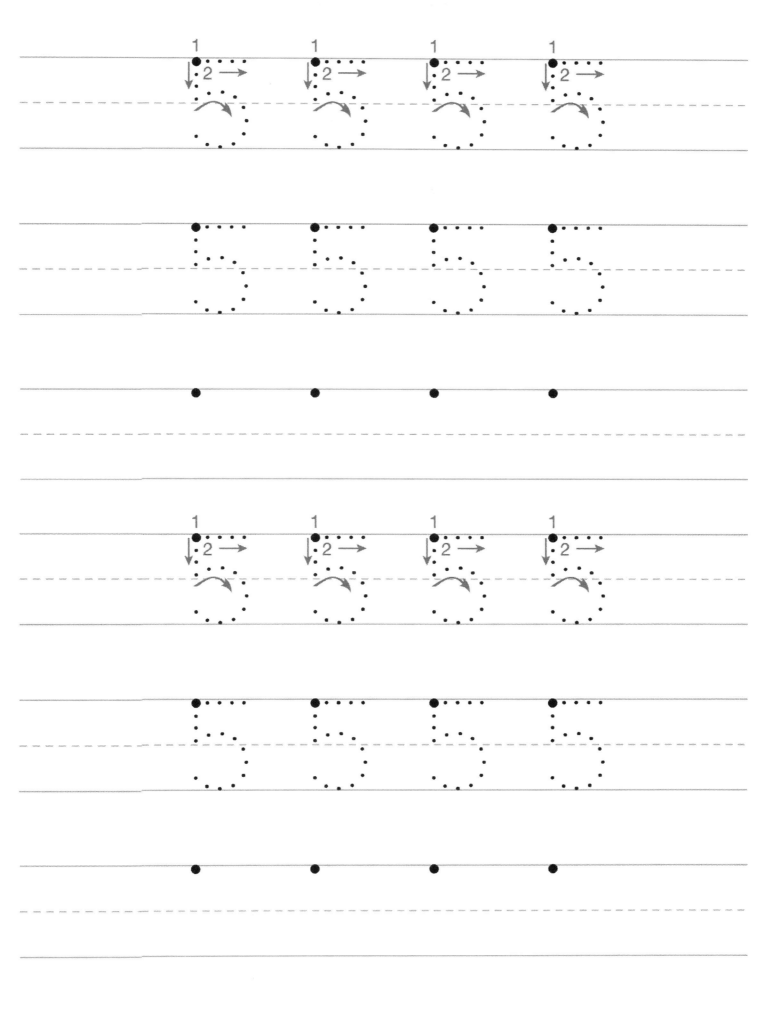

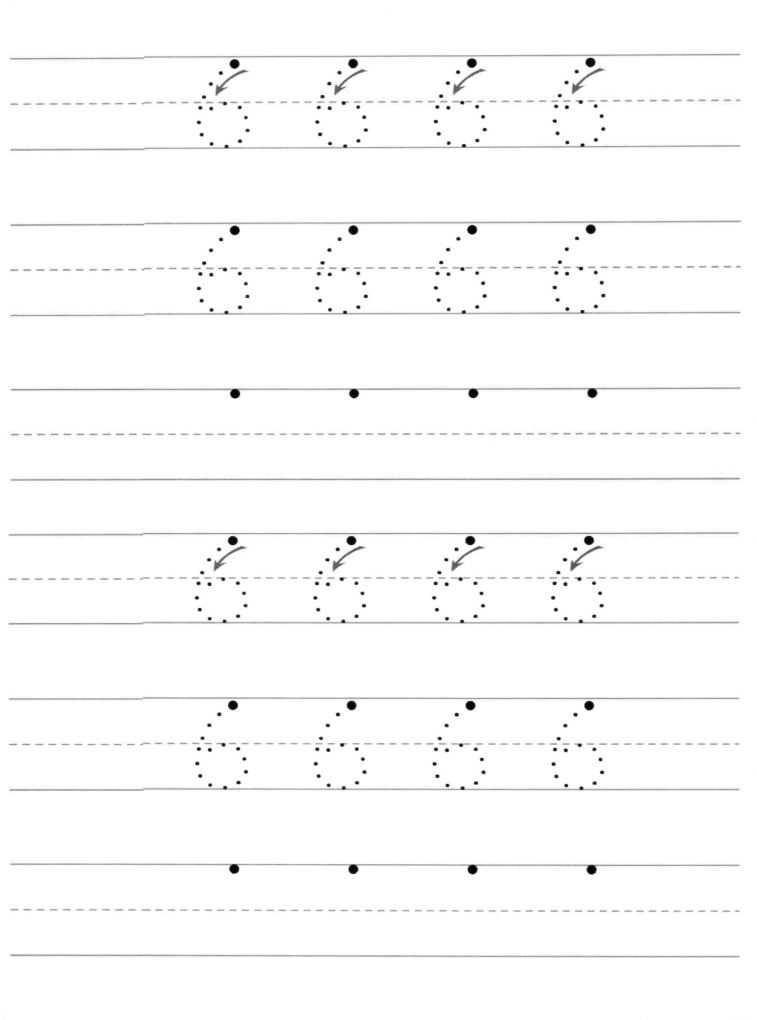

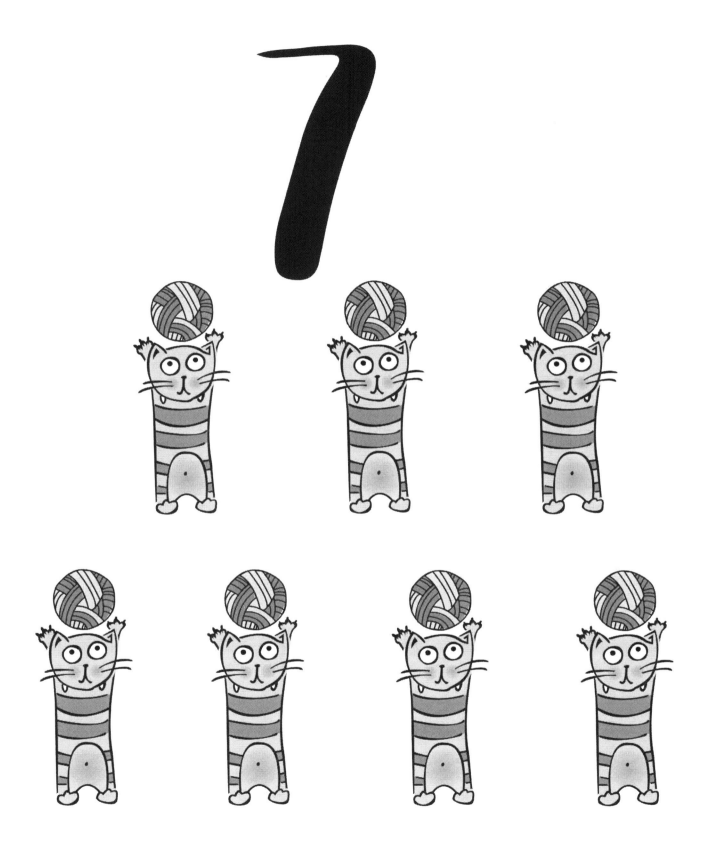

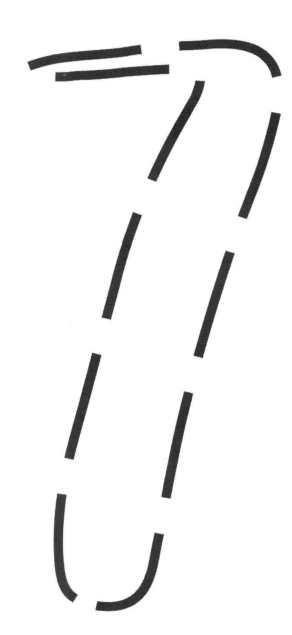

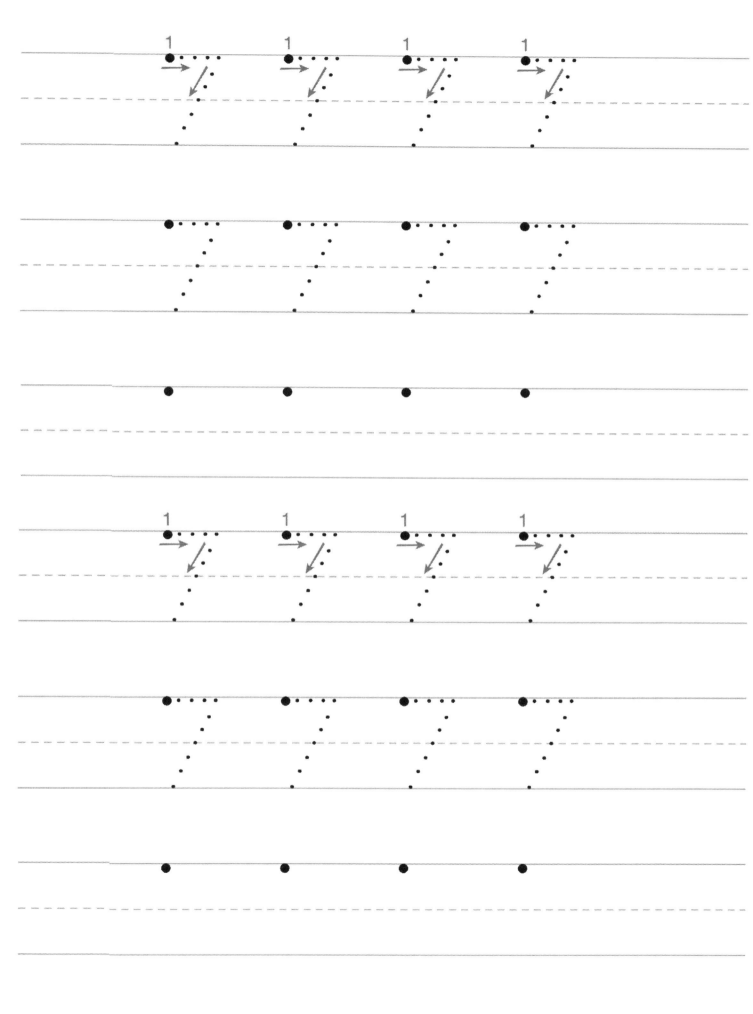

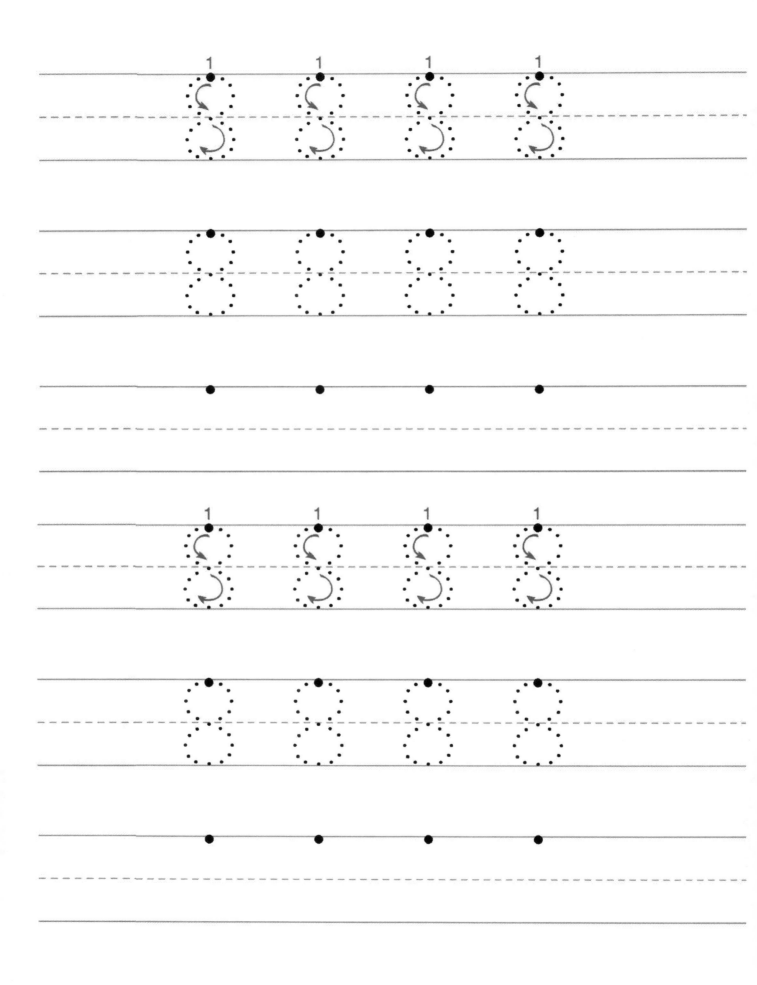

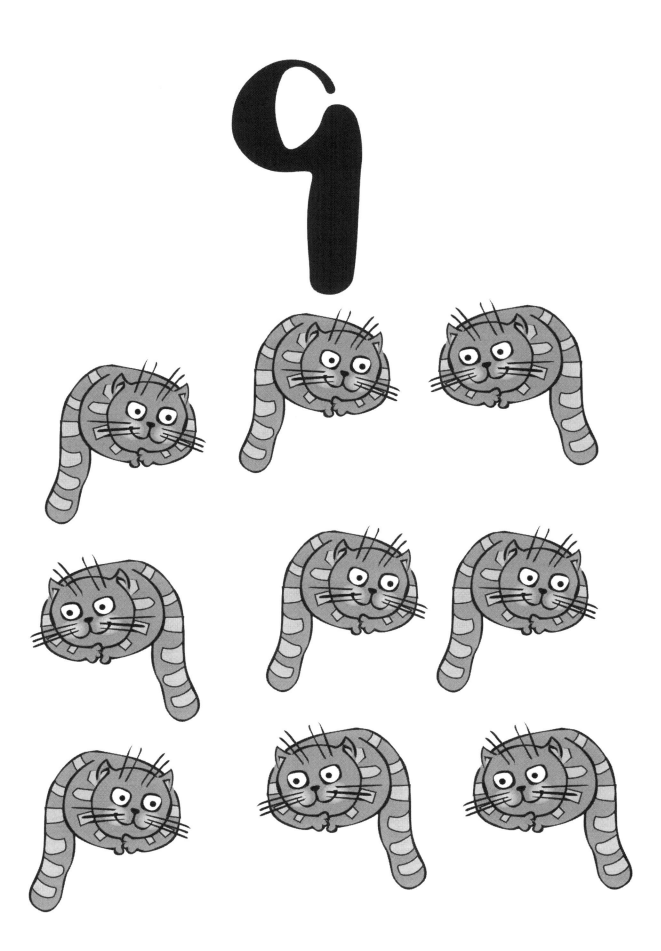

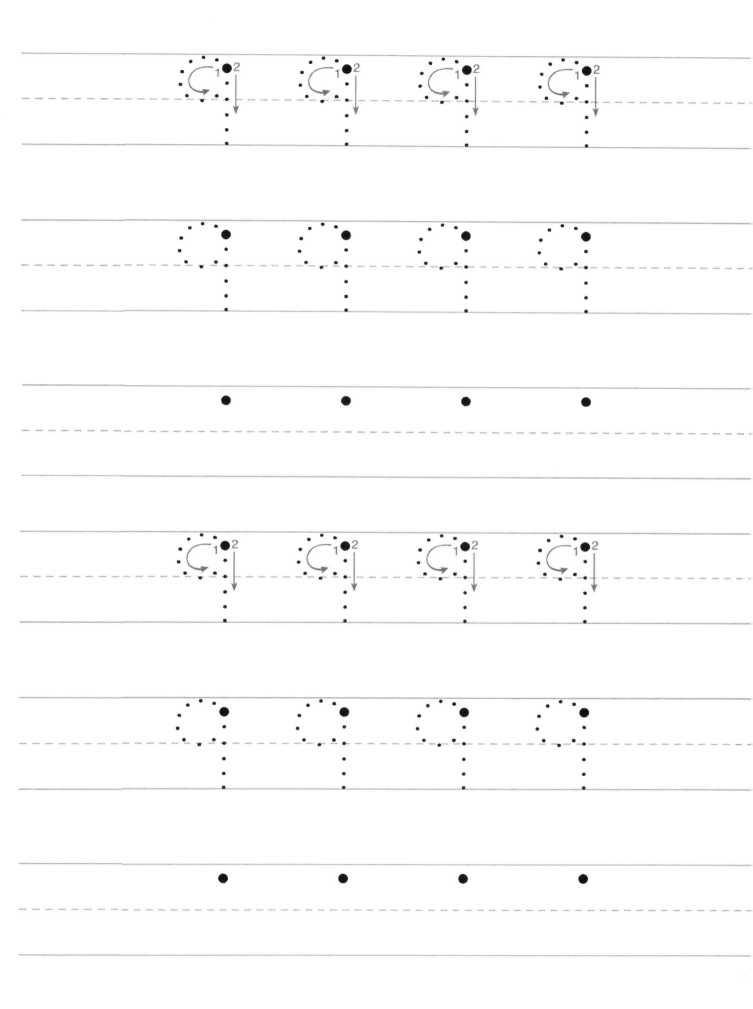

Made in the USA
San Bernardino,
CA